C000004598

BEDFORDS

A CENTURY IN PHOTOGRAPHS

Published jointly by
Bedfordshire Federation of Women's Institutes
and Countryside Books

COUNTRYSIDE BOOKS
3 Catherine Road
Newbury, Berkshire

ISBN 1 85306 449 1

FRONT COVER PHOTOGRAPH OF MR WIN COOK, ON THE ROAD TO WOBURN
SUPPLIED BY MRS R. BROWN, ASPLEY GUISE WI.

BACK COVER PHOTOGRAPH OF MR H. DEAR, OF SHEFFORD
SUPPLIED BY ANNE ROBERTS, HAYNES WI.

Designed by Graham Whiteman

Produced through MRM Associates Ltd., Reading

Printed by Woolnough Bookbinding Ltd., Irthlingborough

CONTENTS

Olive Burgoyne with her mother and young daughter, picnicking on Bradgers Hills 1938.
(Mrs I. Pope – Todding WI)

FOREWORD

After our previous successes with the *Bedfordshire Village Book* and B*edfordshire Within Living Memory*, it was with pleasure that we agreed to participate in this wonderful pictorial record of life and times in our County during this century.

The photographs cover all aspects of our lives, whether it be domestic, work, or drama and demonstrate the changes that have occurred, both in the town and the country, over the years.

I hope this book brings back recollections and memories to all who read it.

Mrs Eileen Parker
County Chairman

ACKNOWLEDGEMENTS

Bedfordshire WI members have again taken up the challenge and provided many delightful and interesting photographs for our latest publication. Unfortunately there has not been space for every photograph submitted but I know that, like myself, members and their families have derived so much pleasure in 'delving and researching'.

My thanks to them all for their contributions to a wonderful pictorial record of life and times in Bedfordshire during this last century.

Mrs Anne Salmon
Co-ordinator

INTO THE 20TH CENTURY

(1900 – 1919)

When the new century began Queen Victoria was still on the throne and Bedfordshire was a county of isolated villages and a few bustling towns, where the unmade roads were often muddy in winter and dusty dry in summer. Most people walked wherever they had to go, and the carrier's cart took them into town for an occasional day's shopping. Bicycles were popular, and there was a thriving cycle-making industry around Biggleswade, but cars were still only for the wealthy. A tramway opened in Luton in 1905.

Bedfordshire's chalk, clay and fertile soil were the basis for its livelihood – in the brick, sand and cement works, particularly in the Stewartby area, or in the chalk quarries in the south. Brewing and market gardening employed many local people. The county's brussels sprouts were famous and produce was sent from here all over the country by rail. The Bedford firm of Laxton was well known for its fruit trees. Horses were still the power on the land, though Bedford had long held a place in the development of agricultural machinery. Boys straight out of school at the age of twelve, if not before, went onto the land or into the quarries; girls had little choice of outside work but to go into service.

An industry from the last century – straw plait and hat making – was still important. Even policemen wore helmets made of straw, and everybody wore a hat when outdoors. In country cottages straw plait was still being made for sale at the Luton market. There were already signs of things to come, however, and a manufacturing base was being laid for the new century. Vauxhall was only one of the several engineering firms to move to Luton in the first decade of the new century.

Country homes were often of stone and thatch, difficult to keep clean and warm, with uneven flagstone floors and no running water, and the privy at the bottom of the garden. Lighting was by candle or oil lamp, or perhaps by gaslight, and in the towns the lamplighter still made his rounds at dawn and at dusk. The first old age pensions were paid in 1909, relieving many old people of the fear of the workhouse.

A day out on a Sunday school or charitable outing was often the only holiday a child could expect away from home. Magic lantern shows were highlights of local entertainment. Annual events such as Bedford Regatta were eagerly awaited. People continued to celebrate the old country festivals too, such as Plough Monday in January, when traditionally the winter ploughing was ended and the men could indulge in horseplay. Empire Day on 24th May was a new holiday for schoolchildren.

Luton Council acquired Wardown Park in 1903. Old estates were being broken up, at Wrest Park, for instance, or Haynes Park in 1914. A swimming pool opened in Luton in 1916, but most children still swam in local rivers.

The century began with Britain at war in South Africa, a conflict in which

1900 – 1919

Bedfordshire men played their part. When war came in 1914 men volunteered immediately, cheered on by friends and relatives. The 51st Highland Scottish Battalion came to Bedford for training. Flying was already becoming important to the county and there were aerodromes at Cardington and Henlow. Two of the King's sons were evacuated for the duration to Ampthill Park, as Lady Ampthill was lady in waiting to Queen Mary. Factories were given over to munitions work.

The end of the war brought both sadness over the 5,000 local men who had died, and relief. The Peace celebrations in Luton in 1919 were marred when a dispute over the involvement of local veterans in the events escalated into a riot and the Town Hall was burned down.

During the war women worked alongside men in the munitions factories and on the land, and kept essential services going. Women over 30 were given the vote after the war, and nearly all public offices and professions opened to them. The war had also been a part of the impetus for the creation of the Women's Institute at this time, encouraging country women to meet, learn and socialise together. The first local Institutes were formed at Shenton and Dunstable in 1917, and the Bedfordshire Federation of Women's Institutes in 1919.

Men from W.T. Sharp, Ampthill Builders in 1908. (Margaret Parrish – Millbrook WI)

Top A scene at the horse fair at Potton c1910, an annual event and a time for buying and selling. There are no women to be seen in this masculine environment.
(Joan Mackey – Silsoe WI)

Centre Silsoe village c1900, with the village policeman looking on. It is a scene untroubled by the motor car.
(Susan Olney – Tingrith WI)

Bottom Mill Lane, Clophill in 1911. The children are carrying small milk cans and were probably off to fetch milk from the local farm after school.
(Mrs J. Izzard – Clophill WI)

Parrott's newsagent's and tobacconist's in Ford End Road, Queens Park, Bedford c1910. Mr Monty Parrott stands to the right with his two sisters, who ran the shop until c1914, in the doorway. The tobacco window was dressed by Mr West of the Imperial Tobacco Company using dummy cigarette packets – the cup shown in the window is thought to be a football trophy.
(Dorothy Warman – Wootton WI)

Russell's General Stores, Shillington Road, Meppershall c1913, with Olive and Tom Russell. Small shops like this were essential for life in the then isolated villages – the shop was in the front corner, with goods in the window, and the living accommodation at the back and far end. A simple lath and plaster building, its corner was often caught by waggons and steam threshing engines, hence the large stones at the foot of the wall and the brick casing on one end. (Frank Russell – c/o Meppershall WI)

S.A. Oliver, butcher, game and poultry dealer at Potton, in front of his impressive Christmas display in 1908. Notices on the carcasses proclaim who the animals were fed by – the turkeys by Mr Tongue, for instance! (Beryl Goodship – Potton WI)

Arthur Neale and his wife Martha outside their baker's shop in High Street, Toddington 1900. The bakehouse was in the cellar, the grating and windows of which can be seen to the right of the doorway. The premises are still used as a bakery today, the business now run by Alan and Jean Childs. (Mrs P. Hart – Toddington WI)

The Meet of the Oakley Hounds at Bromham in February 1908, looking towards Bromham Mill.
(Pam Saunders – Toddington WI)

A. Biggs' furniture removal van, horse-drawn, at Luton in 1911. Alphonso Biggs stands, in the white apron, to the right, while one of his sons, Ernie, stands by the horses. It remained a family firm (with motorised vans) until the 1970s.
(Mr A. Rodell – c/o Flitton & Greenfield WI)

Setting off on a long journey – the Tilzey sisters leaving Toddington en route for Harlington station and Manchester in 1908.
(Mrs R. Williams – Toddington WI)

Charles and Elizabeth Bird of Dunstable Road, Luton on a tandem in the early 1900s. Bicycles were extremely popular forms of transport for both men and women. (Mary Little – Toddington WI)

Below *Said to be the first Ford motor car in Luton, c1911, in the yard of the Wellington Arms with its owner, Walter Burgoyne. The car was later rebuilt as a four-seater.* (Mrs I. Pope – Toddington WI)

The Eyles family of Beech Hill, Luton repairing their bicycles, c1914.
(Jill Thomas – Heath & Reach WI)

One of the first aeroplanes to land in the Luton area, September 1913. It was a Type 38 Short Brothers two-seater pusher biplane attached to the Royal Navy, that had been taking part in Army manoeuvres near Rugby and was returning to the Isle of Sheppey when it ran short of fuel. It came down on fields close to the site of the present Luton Airport and local people flocked to the scene.
(Angela Brown – Flitton & Greenfield WI)

In the yard of the Wellington Arms, Luton c1911, licensee's sons Stanley and Leslie Burgoyne. The picture was sent out with the family's Christmas greetings, so the two lads were dressed in their best clothes. (Mrs I. Pope – Toddington WI)

Before the Women's Institutes were formed there was little opportunity for women to meet, learn and socialise together. At Stondon the local women met at the Mothers' Meeting. This picture was taken c1910, with Mrs Long, the founder, sitting in the centre. The Long family were the local 'squires'. Despite appearances, many of these women would have been of an age today considered young! (Joan Wood –Meppershall WI)

A delightful group of girls at Sharnbrook Council School before 1906. The young teacher on the left was Miss Florence Woods, who was headmistress at schools in Souldrop, Eggington and Leighton Buzzard before her marriage in 1914.
(Mrs G. Head – Wootton WI)

Below Staff at the Girls' *Modern School, Bedford in 1915, which later became the Dame Alice School.*
(Pam Saunders – Toddington WI)

Boys of the Houghton Regis Church Lads' Brigade in 1914. Like other similar organisations, the Brigade sought to instil military discipline and order in working class boys' lives. (Mrs V. Squires – Totternhoe WI)

Hat factory girls in 1917, at Luton. For many decades before this, it had been felt that the money women and girls earned in the straw hat industry locally made them far too independent!
(Susan Olney – Tingrith WI)

Miss Sleeman came to Bedfordshire as nanny to the
Durlers' only child. At that time, 1910, the Durler family
were involved in the hat industry in Luton.
(Peggy Pyrke – Streatley Village WI)

Cowmen who worked for
Mr Patterson of Newbury
Farm, Silsoe. The eldest,
Martin, was killed in the
First World War.
(Susan Olney –
Tingrith WI)

In 1901, a period of rest for
the stack builders at Tithe
Farm, Potton. The boys
were hired to kill the mice
in the fields and to stook
the sheaves. The steam
engine to power the
elevator, and later to do
the threshing, would be
hired out to local farmers,
in this case by T.B.
Kitchener & Co.
(P. Yates – Potton WI)

Top *In May 1900, during the Boer War, people gathered in Potton's Market Square to celebrate the relief of Mafeking. Bells brought people out of their houses to hear the good news.* (Beryl Goodship – Potton WI)

In August 1914 at Potton, tradesmen hired a bus to convey a contingent of volunteers for Lord Kitchener's Army to Biggleswade station. All over the county similar scenes were enacted as men rushed to join up. (Sheila Jarvis – Potton WI)

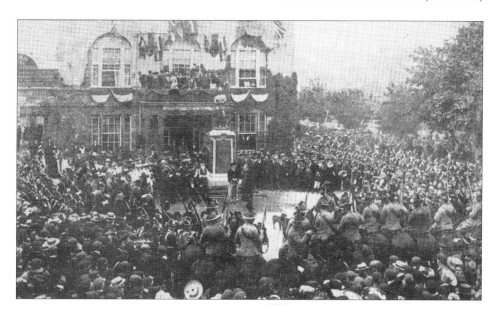

THEN & NOW: On 2nd June 1904, after the war was over, the Soldiers' Memorial was unveiled at Bedford – and today (left) the same spot before the Swan Hotel.
(Christine Bertram – Ravensden WI)

Bottom left Sylvia Newell and Eve Quenby helping with the harvest in the Bromham area at the end of the war. Women had taken on many of the tasks normally performed by men, including work on the land, and this and similar pictures may have been taken as publicity photographs. (Pam Saunders – Toddington WI)

Left Cpl. A. Huchinson visiting former workmates whilst on leave in 1916. The field where they were working was known as Oak Piece, on the Sutton border with Potton. (PHS Collection – Potton WI)

Men and women at work in a munitions factory during the First World War, probably in the Luton area. (Jill Thomas – Heath & Reach WI)

Between The Wars

(1920 – 1938)

Bedfordshire was less severely hit by the industrial depression between the wars than the North of England, though agriculture struggled for survival during these years. The Jarrow Marchers stopped at Goldington Road School in Bedford on their way to London, a sharp reminder of the misery many were suffering in the rest of the country.

Bedfordshire's new industries continued to grow, based on electricity not coal, and concentrating on consumer goods and commodities in great demand, such as bricks for house building. At Leighton Buzzard they produced a range of goods from sand to Gossard's corsets. Blue Circle Cement built their works at Houghton Regis, where the land is rich in chalk, in 1930. Car ownership was growing and Luton's Vauxhall factory was at the forefront of development – and there were still thousands of men and women employed in the old hat industry in the town.

It was the heyday of the village and corner shop. Tradesmen began to change from horse and cart to motorised van, but they still called for orders every week at the door. Errand boys on bikes were to be found in every town, usually whistling the latest tunes.

The radio was our link with the world of music, drama, news and humour, from the early crystal sets to the cabinet-enclosed wirelesses. Cinemas drew huge audiences for the latest films – silent at first but then increasingly sophisticated 'talkies'.

Whipsnade Zoo opened in 1931, intended at first merely as a peaceful country retreat for the animals at London Zoo!

Village schools had changed very little. Tortoise stoves or open fires for heating, earth closets and no running water, chalk dust and inkwells, the cane and the Three Rs were all part of children's experience of education. Children played games in the roads or out in the fields, with little equipment but a lot of imagination. It was normal to be out all day away from home in the summer holidays, and parents gave it little thought or concern.

Clothes were becoming lighter and easier to wear, though hats were still essential outdoor wear. Women worked only until they married, if they worked at all, though in this generation of women, so many had lost their loved ones in the war. Servants were still in demand in upper and middle class homes.

On the land, horses were beginning to lose the battle with mechanisation as the first tractors appeared in the fields. Many families were able to afford their first car, and roads began to get busier.

Flying caught the public imagination between the wars. The giant airship sheds at Cardington became a landmark. In 1930 the crash of the R101 airship in France appalled the nation and 150,000 people lined the route of the funeral procession in Bedfordshire as they mourned the crew and passengers. Richard Shuttleworth of Old Warden started his collection of cars in 1928 and then of aeroplanes in 1935. The

1920 – 1938

The boys of
Clophill School at
work in the school
garden, c1936.
The school has
since been
demolished and a
modern school
built on the site.
(Mrs J. Izzard –
Clophill WI)

'Flying Duchess' – Mary, Duchess of Bedford – lost her life while flying. During the 1920s one of the founders of de Havilland lived and farmed at Studham and flew his plane to the factory at Hatfield.

As early as 1933 Luton Borough Council were determined that London's northern airport would be here. They bought the land at Buttermilk Hill for £149,000, and in 1936 the Perceval Aircraft Company began making planes there. In 1938 Luton Airport opened as a Class A aerodrome, and the record-breaking flier Amy Johnson was one of the celebrity attractions on opening day.

The Square at Aspley Guise c1920. It has changed very little today though there is no longer a grocer's shop or a bakery, and the horse trough has been replaced by a central traffic island and a shelter. On the right of the scene today is the Moore Place Hotel.
(Mrs R. Brown –Aspley Guise WI)

Mrs Martha Deverick in 1920, outside her daughter's home at Church Walk, Kempston, in the area still known as Bell End. She attended the nearby Methodist chapel.
(Dorothy Warman – Wootton WI)

Left *W.H. Fowler, landlord at the Rose and Crown 1930.*
(Joan Mackey – Silsoe WI)

Biscot Windmill, Luton c1930. A smock mill that had replaced a post mill in the 1840s, it was pulled down in the late 1930s. A public house was built on the site – The Biscot Mill – and the area is still referred to as Biscot Mill or simply as The Mill, where five roads meet. (Mrs I. Pope – Toddington WI)

Below – left and right.
The river Ouse at Bedford
c1928. The river was a
popular place for Sunday
outings. There were small
pleasure steamers, for river
cruises, and many rowing
boats for hire.
(Angela Brown –
Flitton & Greenfield
WI)

THEN & NOW: In the 1920s Mr Francis Fletcher farmed a new smallholding at Limbury and named it Mead Farm. He worked the farm on his own, only employing extra help at harvest. His main crop was wheat and each year he took a sample to Mr Tooley, the miller at Biscot Mill, who offered him a price according to the quality. A bad harvest was a great disappointment. Today the farmhouse is part of Icknield Way, surrounded by Limbury Mead Estate, Luton.

(Angela Brown – Flitton & Greenfield WI)

A house of very modern design in Old Bedford Road, Luton 1935, near Elmwood Crescent. It is still there today, known locally as the 'Sunshine' or 'Seaside' house.
(Mrs I. Pope
–Toddington WI)

Charles Bird bought this
car from the Duke of
Bedford, and used it for
outings in the Woburn
area in 1922.
(Mary Little –
Toddington WI)

Olive Theobald of Luton at the wheel of an Austin 7 at Clophill in 1928 – motoring was becoming a part of everyday life now.
(Mrs I. Pope – Toddington WI)

Cars waiting in Williamson Street, Luton in the 1920s – part of a procession of vehicles taking 'poor crippled children on an outing to the fairground at Bricket Wood.
(Mrs I. Pope – Toddington WI)

Village bobby PC Armstrong, outside 8 Rectory Road, Meppershall in 1925. This was rented as the police house from c1910 until the police built their own house in Shefford Road in 1927. There is no local policeman stationed in the village today, and the police house was sold in the 1960s.
(Joan Wood – Meppershall WI)

Members of Potton Volunteer Fire Brigade were called to Home Farm in 1935. The farm was owned by the Land Settlement Association, which bought 713 acres locally to settle unemployed men from the North-East.
(Beryl Goodship – Potton WI)

Hay time 1924 at Clipstone. The hay was pitched from the tumbrel cart on to the elevator, taking the hay up to a rick being built by one or two men. This normally took place near the farm in a rickyard, and the hay was then kept for winter feed. The sweet scent of freshly cut hay was a part of summer.
(Mrs G. Calder – Eggington WI)

Arthur Hull of Keysoe, working at Buryfields Farm c1925. Like most boys, he left school at 14, and then began work by helping his uncle on the farm until he was old enough to do an apprenticeship in Bedford as a motor mechanic. The farm is still there today, though no one has lived there for 30 years. (Sheila Pope – Keysoe WI)

Cleaning Staploe Brook in the 1920s. The brook would get overgrown with vegetation, flooding out on to the road. George Carter and Joe Ball were local men who worked for Mr Squire, and the old gentleman sitting on the fence is Mr Ford.
(Freda Hawkins – Keysoe WI)

A forestry gang of the early 1920s. This section of men on the Duke of Bedford's estate were responsible for the forestry in Ampthill, Millbrook, Lidlington and Steppingley. Mr Doulton, at the back in the trilby hat, was the overseer of the gang.
(Margaret Parrish – Millbrook WI)

Bob Wheatley with his dog and gun, at Sharnbrook 1920.
One of his duties on the farm was to act as gamekeeper.
(Sheila Pope – Keysoe WI)

Elstow May Day 1938. A blanket is being held to collect the money thrown by spectators.
(Sheila Pope – Keysoe WI)

King George V and Queen Mary at Bedford High School in 1926, opening the new Science block.
(Pam Saunders – Toddington WI)

Crowds in New Bedford Road, at the junction of Alexander Avenue, Luton after the procession which formed part of the festivities for George V's Silver Jubilee in 1935.
(Mrs S. Coleman – Caddington WI)

George VI's coronation in 1937 saw street parties and sports all over the county. The inhabitants of Garfield Street, Bedford got together to provide a tea for the children.
(Jane Allen – Wootton WI)

41

Silsoe football team, 1921, made up of village lads – just one of the village sides in the county.
(Susan Olney – Tingrith WI)

The Luton Town team at the railway station in 1933, the year they won the Cup-tie against Tottenham Hotspur.
(Joan Mackey – Silsoe WI)

Left & Right *Luton Town football team at a private practice match at Luton Town football ground in August 1932, and playing a match in January 1933.*
(Joan Mackey – Silsoe WI)

Pupils of Church End School, in Kempston Rural, 1921. The school is still there today and celebrated its 150th anniversary in the 1990s.
(Dorothy Warman – Wootton WI)

Local workmen at Cardington Camp in 1938, building huts for the RAF intake base which became so important when war broke out a year later.
(Sheila Pope – Keysoe WI)

Right *There was a great sense of personal loss when the R101 airship crashed in France in 1930. The bodies of the victims were brought back to Cardington by special train. 'My husband recalls as a young boy being taken to the railway line near Aspley Guise where people were lining the tracks as the train slowly passed.'*
(Mrs C. Cox – Haynes WI; Doreen Brown – Aspley Guise WI)

The R100 airship at Cardington in the 1920s. There was great interest in the airships in the local area and many people came to see them.
(Mrs R. Brown – Aspley Guise WI)

The R100 in flight over Cardington.
(Mrs I. Pope – Toddington WI)

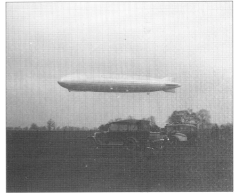

THE SECOND WORLD WAR

(1939 – 1945)

War was declared on Sunday, 3rd September 1939 and three days later the first air raid siren sounded at Bedford. Yet little happened at first and people began to talk of a 'phoney war'. Trenches were dug in Luton, Bedford and Dunstable as air raid shelters, and families later issued with Anderson or Morrison shelters to use in their gardens or homes. Luton Airport was camouflaged. Gas masks were to be carried at all times, with Mickey Mouse faces for young children. Windows were criss-crossed with tape to prevent them shattering in a blast, and the blackout was strictly enforced.

Over 35,000 evacuees arrived in the county from London and the South Coast, mostly children who were feared to be at risk if and when the bombing began. This was much to the annoyance of Luton authorities, who argued that the several thousand who were sent to the town were as much at risk in this industrial centre as they were at home!

Businesses were relocated from London to the peace of Bedford, as was part of the BBC, who continued to broadcast from their new home. Woburn Abbey was taken over by the Government, and Ampthill Park requisitioned as a hospital. Vauxhall's made Churchill tanks.

Events at Dunkirk brought home to us how quickly the invasion of Britain had become a possibility. On 26th June 1940 the first bombs fell on the county, near the village of Pertenhall, and more rapidly followed. Luton suffered the most, from August 1940 when with the first, and worst, raid of the war 200 bombs fell on the town. Bedfordshire's very last bomb of the war was a V2 rocket, which fell at Studham and killed twelve people.

Airfields were soon in operation, the roar of British and American bombers becoming a familiar sound. Luton was taken over by the Air Ministry. Cardington was a reception area for recruits and produced barrage balloons. From Tempsford, the RAF dropped agents and equipment into German-occupied Europe. Leighton Buzzard was the headquarters for RAF Signals, and the RAF were also based at Chicksands, near Shefford. Cranfield, Thurleigh and Little Staughton were new stations, created with long runways specially for the use of the RAF and USAF. Half the village of Little Staughton had to go to make the space. Henlow was said at one time to be the largest RAF station in England. Bomber Command was based in the Whipsnade area. Polish pilots were based at Thurleigh, and in 1942 the American Eighth Army Air Force arrived with their Flying Fortresses. The Americans, with their easy generosity, unrationed food and nylon stockings were quickly absorbed into local life!

The civilian population was fully involved, from taking in evacuees and servicemen to serving voluntarily in local organisations and services. The Home Guard brought together the young, old and those in reserve occupations; there were eight battalions in the county, based at Ampthill, Bedford, Biggleswade, Dunstable

1939 – 1945

Bikes were essential transport for the many American servicemen stationed in Bedfordshire – here at Thurleigh Airfield. (Sheila Pope – Keysoe WI)

and Luton. Other men and women served as air raid wardens or firefighters, or went into munitions factories. The Women's Land Army supplemented the labour force on the land, essential when every spare foot of land was used for growing food and we were being urged to 'dig for victory'. The Women's Institutes took a very active role in providing information, advice and support to local communities. The Bedfordshire Federation's 25th anniversary had to pass uncelebrated in 1944.

Then at last it was over. Street parties and bonfires celebrated VE Day in May 1945, with hoarded goodies brought out to give children a day to remember and the return of loved ones to look forward to.

47

A B17 Flying Fortress named Ass Bandits, *with the bomb-loading crew from 423 Squadron sitting on top.*

Thurleigh Airfield was used by the RAF, the Polish Air Force, and, most notably to the locals, the American Eighth Air Force. It became Station 111, home to the 306th Bombardment Group (H), comprising four squadrons – 367 (Clay Pigeons), 368 (Eager Beavers), 369 (Grim Reapers) and 423 (Fitin' Bitin'). They arrived in July 1942, and were the first Americans to bomb Germany, on 9th October – hence their slogan 'First Over Germany'. They did not leave until May 1945. (Sheila Pope – Keysoe WI)

John Krische, Nick Etter, Jack Lazer and Jim Robinson of 432 Squadron based at Thurleigh, with some of the bombs that were stored in Pippin Wood, Riseley under camouflage netting. (Sheila Pope – Keysoe WI)

Members of Meppershall Home Guard 1942. Units like this were raised all over the country, formed from men too old or too young for active service, or who were engaged in vital war work. They are best known today for their Dad's Army image, but at the time were ready and willing to defend their country to the last man. (Joan Wood – Meppershall WI)

49

The ladies of the Women's Voluntary Services Mobile Canteen, at Bromham 1945. 'The Bromham group was run by a Mrs Foulkes, and we took the canteen to Twinwood's Airfield every day. Pat Gilbert (the other young one) and I always did Saturdays as we were working during the week, and we would be invited to the dance in the canteen, to which we always cycled five or six miles.' (Pam Saunders – Toddington WI)

Right Peggy, Rene, Phyllis and Freda, land girls, at Staploe 1942. Ensuring that food production was maintained was vital war work and girls from all walks of life were called up, or volunteered, for the Women's Land Army. Peggy came from London but the other three of the group were local – Rene from Little Staughton, Phyllis from Eynesbury and Freda from Duloe – and all of them stayed in the area after the war, two marrying farmers from Keysoe. 'We spent many cold wintry days in this large glasshouse sorting the seed potatoes, weighing and stacking for Mr Noel Bates.' (Freda Hawkins – Keysoe WI)

A fete in the Rectory garden at Meppershall in 1944, with sailor Jack Harris running the hoop-la stall.
(Joan Wood – Meppershall WI)

Prisoners of war were housed in many places in the county, with camps at Dunstable (the London Gliding Club), near Luton Airport (for Italians) and in Ampthill Park (for Germans). The Italians wore a distinctive brown uniform with coloured patches on the back for easy identification. They worked on the farms, and were reasonably treated and fed. A Flitwick resident remembers the lorries taking them through Marston Moretaine each morning and the wooden toys they made. 'This young German POW was walking by the river in Bedford just after the war in 1946 and asked us to take his photograph. He was friendly and seemed pleased to be here.' (Angela Brown – Flitton & Greenfield WI)

Right Workers from the factory of Charles Clay & Sons in 1942, wearing the bib and brace overalls made at the factory – they took part in the War Workers Parade at Luton on 14th June 1942, which was followed by a service held at Luton Town football ground.
(Mrs S. Coleman – Caddington WI)

Children from heavily bombed areas found homes in the Bedfordshire countryside. Young Philip came from London to Clipstone, where he lived in safety on the Batchelar family farm. Here he was in 1941 playing happily with Janet and Guinevere Batchelar on an International tractor. (Guinevere Calder – Eggington WI)

Valentine Olney, butcher of 12 High Street, Silsoe, in 1940. Mr Olney kept his own hens and ten cows. He used the coupons he got for the produce he sold in his shop to get food for his animals, rationing affecting animals as well as people. (Susan Olney – Tingrith WI)

Evacuees were not always children – these two sisters were evacuated to Luton after their house in Bromley was bombed. Miss Brown (right) was buried under the rubble for several hours before being rescued and always wore her hair in this way, to hide the scar on her forehead from her injuries. They are remembered as kind, gentle people. (Angela Brown – Flitton & Greenfield WI)

The kind of country scene that meant so much at this time of war – the corner of Stondon Lane c1940, with children Joan and Barbara Jackson standing with their grandparents outside their cottage. (Joan Wood – Meppershall WI)

A wartime wedding at St Martin's church, Bedford. Frederick Howse married Molly Bates in April 1942 while home on leave, and they were attended by Molly's fellow WAAFs, stationed at Holton Camp. Frederick was in the Blood Transfusion Unit and went over with the D-Day landings in 1944. Organising a wedding in wartime was not easy, as food and clothing were strictly rationed, but usually friends and family would rally round to provide the essentials and to make the day one to remember.
(Jane Allen – Wootton WI)

VE Day at Luton, with a joint celebration for the residents of Cranleigh Gardens and Fountains Road. It was organised by the butcher's wife Mrs Thody (the buxom lady in the photograph). There was a fancy dress parade, a talent competition and a bonfire with a Nazi flag and an effigy of Hitler on top.
(Angela Brown – Flitton & Greenfield WI)

THE POST-WAR YEARS

(1946 – 1959)

It was still a world of austerity and shortages, with bread not coming off ration until 1948 and some foods still strictly controlled into the 1950s. We entered a nuclear age, but coal was on ration until 1958. The bleak winter of 1947 seemed to epitomise the hardships of post-war life.

Great social changes took place as men and women used their vote to demand a better way of life. The National Health Service began in 1948, and essential public services such as water and electricity were nationalised by the post-war Labour government.

New homes were urgently needed to replace those lost or damaged by bombing, and Bedford's bricks and building materials were in demand. There were vast brickworks to the south of Bedford and around Biggleswade. London Brickworks' big kiln at Stewartby took a year to reheat after its closure during the war when the great chimney was considered a target for enemy planes.

Country estates were again under threat and some found new uses as schools or colleges. Richard Ormonde Shuttleworth was killed serving in the RAF and in his memory his estate was put into trust for the teaching of aviation, agriculture and forestry. Luton acquired Stockwood Park in 1945. In 1955, the Duke of Bedford became the first great landowner to 'sell' his house to the general public when the doors of Woburn Abbey were opened to paying customers.

The bulk of the county was still rural, though Bedford, Dunstable and Luton held about half the county's population between them. There was a continuing drift away from the land by young people, and land girls and prisoners of war were still to be seen working on farms and market gardens some years after the war's end.

More cars and buses on the roads brought commuters to the county. In 1959 the M1 was opened, the country's first motorway, and ushered in a new age of road travel. Already concerns were being voiced about increasing traffic – except perhaps in Luton's expanding motor industry!

'London overspill' families were housed at Houghton Regis. Immigrants from overseas also came to Bedfordshire to live and work – from Italy, the Caribbean, India, Pakistan and Poland – most of them settling in Bedford and Luton in the brick and engineering industries.

Luton Airport expanded rapidly, a new concrete runway completed by 1960 to cope with the expected increase in passenger traffic. Cranfield became the home of the College of Aeronautical Engineering, while Thurleigh's wartime airfield formed the nucleus of the Royal Aircraft Establishment. Henlow and Chicksands remained active service units.

Luton Town Football Club delighted the town by remaining in the First Division from 1955 to 1959, and reaching the Cup Final.

More women went out to work and

were not content to merely go back into service – the days of the servant were past. Consumer goods began to appear in more homes. Television took its hold on family life, though cinemas were still fighting back for our custom. The familiar red telephone kiosks seemed to be appearing in even the most remote rural areas, and home telephones also spread. Libraries came to the villages, and museums opened in Luton and Bedford. Nationally, the

Women's Institute bought their own residential college at Denham in Oxfordshire in 1945 and opened it to students in 1948, many women taking the opportunity for training and education.

Queen Elizabeth II's coronation was celebrated with street parties throughout the county in June 1953. With opportunities opening up for ordinary people in education, travel and jobs, it did seem fair to see this as the start of a new Elizabethan Age.

An early combine harvester in 1955. 'A neighbour, Richard Stangton, bought an early type to do contracting. It meant two men could do the work of a gang in one operation.' (Pam Saunders – Toddington WI)

*Mrs Sarah Pope and Mrs
Mynott, on the bicycle,
catching up with local
news on Riseley High
Street.*
(Sheila Pope – Keysoe
WI)

THEN & NOW. On the New Bedford Road in Luton in the early 1950s with just one Austin Ten in sight. The fire station was built on the land to the left, and opened in July 1956. (Angela Brown – Flitton & Greenfield WI)

Keysoe war memorial in the early 1950s, a remembrance service with the Royal British Legion and the WI choir. The war still felt very close at such times.
(Sheila Pope – Keysoe WI)

At the corner of Northwood End Road, Haynes in the 1950s. The cottage on the corner disappeared many years ago and the wooden shop known as 'Jim's' was finally demolished in 1996, and two new houses now stand on the corner.
(Mo Smith – Haynes WI)

The Hertfordshire Hounds at Silsoe, 1948. Charlie Samways was Huntsman from 1930 and latterly his brother whipped in for him. Col D.C. Part was a former Master from Houghton Hall, Houghton Regis, where the Hunt kennels were. From 1948 Lt Col R.C. Faulconer and the Hon Mrs J.F. Harrison were Joint Masters. They hunted three days a week, Monday, Wednesday and Saturday. The Hertfordshire Hounds were disbanded in 1970, and amalgamated with the Old Berkley and South Oxfordshire to form the Vale of Aylesbury Hunt.
(Joan Mackey – Silsoe WI)

Dances were held in many village halls every Saturday. The Swallow Dance Band, which played every week in Wilden village hall, was unique in that the pianist and lady accordion player were both blind. Many romances began at the local dance.
(Sheila Pope – Keysoe WI)

John Skeaping's 'Stallion' was on display at Whipsnade Zoo from 1937 to 1947. It is now in the Tate Gallery.
(Angela Brown – Flitton & Greenfield WI)

Mrs Gammon of Mill Road, Thurleigh working at her lace in the late 1940s. Like many women, she had a large family and to supplement her farm worker husband's wages she made Bedfordshire Pillow Lace. This was sold to Braggins in Bedford, sent with the weekly carrier. She lived in this thatched cottage all her married life.
(Sheila Pope – Keysoe WI)

At Luton Hoo in the early 1950s, waiting for Winston Churchill to speak. He was in his second term as Prime Minister, and had come to give a party 'pep talk'.
(Pam Saunders – Toddington WI)

Keysoe school infants' class in 1948.
(Sheila Pope – Keysoe WI)

The May Day parade.
(Anne Roberts – Haynes WI)

Left *When the bells were hung in Silsoe church in 1951. The five original bells were rehung and a Treble added to make six; Mr Tom Harris OBE was the Ringing Master then and is still Ringing Master in 1997.*
(Susan Olney – Tingrith WI)

Below *Residents of Beale Street, Dunstable celebrating the 1953 Coronation.* (Jill Stubbs – Houghton Regis WI)

Just after the war much of the work on the land was still being done by a combination of older men, POWs and land girls. This was the workforce at College Farm, Oakley in 1946.
(Pam Saunders – Toddington WI)

German prisoners of war sawing logs at Eggington during the severe winter of 1947. Fuel was still in scarce supply so soon after the war and trees were felled to provide wood for home fires. These POWs had arrived after the war and stayed about two years before returning to Germany. They lived in a converted loft at the farmhouse and were very strong men – one made a forge and bellows and used it to make a trailer and to repair farm implements.
(Mrs G. Calder – Eggington WI)

Haystacking and cornstacking at Clay End Farm, Sutton in the 1940s. Horses were still part of the workforce on many farms, and the craft of stacking an essential element of the harvesting scene.
(Mary Leonard – Dunton WI)

THE POST-WAR YEARS (1946–1959)

*The Simkins family of Chapel Farm, Meppershall
delivered milk from the 1920s to the late 1950s – latterly
their deliveries were made in this Morris Oxford van.
Before the war the horse-drawn milk float carrying churns
and measures was a more familiar sight – this was the
Wiles' float of Keeley End Farm, Wootton in the 1930s.*
(Donald Simkins- c/o Meppershall WI; June Wiles
– Wootton WI)

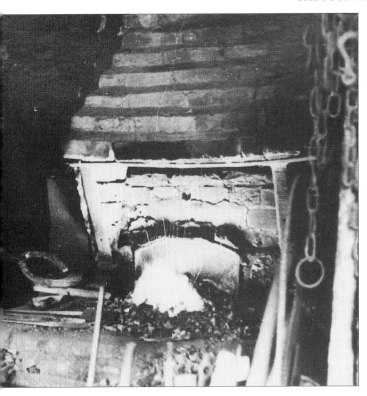

Mr E.F. Smith of The Forge, Brook End, Potton was a shoeing and general blacksmith, specialising in repairing and making agricultural implements. Horseshoes were always displayed on the walls of his shop. He retired in 1965.
(PHS – Potton WI)

The new excavator brought into the London Brick Company's works at Stewartby c1950. The pit where it worked, one of the largest in the country at the time, is now known as Stewartby Lake. LBC have been in the area since 1897; before that the firm was known as Forders and until 1936 it was LBC & Forders.
(Mrs M. Keep – Marston Moreteyne WI)

71

Looking from Dunstable Road, Houghton Regis towards the Blue Circle cement works, with Townsend Farm on the right. A second chimney was built in the 1960s, causing some unpleasant side effects which included covering local roofs and gardens with white ash. The works are now dismantled and the area where the chalk was dug out is a nature reserve.
(Mrs J. Cheshire – Houghton Regis WI)

Vauxhall Motors celebrated their Golden Jubilee in 1953. 'My grandfather, Mr Edwin Horne, is shown sitting in the driving seat of the 1903 vehicle. This was the first Vauxhall car offered for sale, at a price of 130 guineas, and was built at the Vauxhall Iron Works Co Ltd factory in Wandsworth Road, London, two years before the move to Luton in 1905 (Vauxhall Motors was not founded until 1907). Prior to the Golden Jubilee in 1953, the original car was traced and found rusting in a barn. It was bought for a large sum and restored. Vauxhall apprentices made many of the replacement parts. When complete, the veteran was displayed alongside the 'latest model', the Velox of 1953.' (Angela Brown – Flitton & Greenfield WI)

The launch of the E-Type Vauxhall at Luton in 1952. (Mrs V. Squires – Totternhoe WI)

THE SIXTIES AND SEVENTIES

(1960 – 1979)

The 'Swinging Sixties' brought changes in music, dance, dress and family life. It was the age of the pop star, the mini skirt, Mary Quant and Twiggy. Youth became everything, and the age of majority was reduced in 1968 from 21 to 18 years. Television and private telephones were to be found in most homes and by now all but the very rural dwellings had the luxury of electricity and indoor sanitation. Though the 1970s were to see bitter strikes and the Three Day Week, for a time anything seemed possible. Concorde made its maiden flight in 1969, and the same year we watched on television as man took his first step on the moon.

New industries were attracted to areas within easy reach of London. By 1961 Luton's population was over a third of the county total. Holidays abroad began to be commonplace, and Luton Airport's passengers could be numbered in the millions. However, there were some doubts about the airport's future and plans for a new terminal had to be shelved while talks went on about the location of London's Third Airport. For a time a huge marquee was used to help cope with the sheer numbers of passengers.

Rail travel was not so fortunate. Dr Beeching's axe fell on branch lines all over the country and rural areas never quite recovered from the loss of their local halt or station.

Road haulage was increasingly taking over from the railways in industry. In Leighton Buzzard in 1919 a light railway network had been built to take sand to the main London & North Western Railway freight yards, but now sand was being taken to its customers by road and in 1967 the sidings were closed. Enthusiasts immediately banded together to preserve the line and today the Leighton Buzzard Narrow Gauge Railway is a popular local attraction.

Decimal currency replaced pounds, shillings and pence in 1971, and two years later Britain joined the Common Market. Supermarkets began to revolutionise the way we shopped, and village life came under threat as small stores and post offices struggled to compete. Village schools, too, faced closure as large comprehensives took in children from wider catchment areas.

Bedfordshire was reluctantly in the headlines in 1961 when the notorious A6 Murder case took place. Petty crook James Hanratty was convicted of the murder of Michael Gregson in a layby on the A6 at Deadmans Hill, south of Bedford, and was executed at Bedford Prison in 1962. Doubts about the case continue to be debated to this day.

In 1967 Bedfordshire's first WI Market was formed and held behind the County Office in St Cuthbert Street, Bedford. Two years later was the Bedfordshire Federation's Golden Jubilee year, and in 1971 they were able, with the help of a generous member, to purchase their own house in Adelaide Square, Bedford. The Diamond Jubilee of Bedfordshire's Women's Institutes was celebrated in 1979.

1960 – 1979

A WI outing to RAF
Chicksands in June 1972,
with Sgt Raymond
Griffin of the Fire
Department. Chicksands
was always 'open house'
to groups and WI
members – Streatley
Village WI members held
a number of evenings
there. Today Chicksands
is deserted. (Peggy
Pyrke – Streatley
Village WI)

The dangers of heavy traffic were vividly highlighted when an accident devastated the centre of Westoning village in September 1976. A petrol tanker was entering the village when the driver braked and skidded, ending up overturning the vehicle. The tanker exploded and the flames spread rapidly to nearby buildings. Luckily no one was killed. The village hall was opened up as an emergency centre to provide food and hot drinks for villagers and emergency workers. (Westoning WI)

Riseley High Street when it was flooded from the brook in the early 1960s. The picture shows Jock Westley on horseback, carrying Susan Hancock safely through, while a group of boys looks on enviously and behind them Mrs Seabon surveys the scene outside her shop, now 70 High Street.
(Mrs G. Head – Wootton WI)

THE SIXTIES AND SEVENTIES (1960–1979)

THEN & NOW. Potton station in 1900, with station staff and the postman, T. Impey, waiting on the canopied platform for the Cambridge to Bedford train. On 30th December 1967, a Saturday night, railway enthusiasts packed the last trains to run on the line, which had opened on 7th July 1862.
(Patricia Yates & Beryl Howe – Potton WI)

A traditional gypsy caravan at Cardington in the mid 1960s.
(Jane Allen – Wootton WI)

Below *Charlie Lucas of Hassett Street, Bedford, who delivered fruit and vegetables in Kempston and Wootton in the 1960s. His horse was kept in a field off Manton Lane, now occupied by the Bedford Modern School.*
(Jane Allen – Wootton WI)

A local industry – inside the tanning department at F.W. Braybrooks in Potton, 1965. At this time the workforce numbered 100, and with its associates the firm had become one of the major tanneries of the world. Over 120,000 skins were processed every year, and in 1967 the firm won the Queen's Award for Industry. Due to lack of space for expansion, the Potton site closed in 1972, the workforce transferring to Hitchin in Hertfordshire.
(Potton WI)

Rugby Cement Works came to Kensworth in 1964 after the closure of their Totternhoe works. Chalk is excavated from four faces, each up to ten metres high; it is conveyed away by an underground pipeline, 57 miles long.

Sometimes the pipe bursts and can make summer look like winter by coating everything with white slurry, as it did at Tebworth in 1976.
(Mrs I. Miller – Houghton Regis WI)

THEN & NOW. Despite the 30 years that separates them, and increasing mechanisation on the farm, the men working on the threshers in these two photographs would have had no difficulty setting to work together. The earlier picture is of Alf Shepherd at Pegsdon Common Farm in the 1940s, the other shows David and Harold Kitchener, Alf Redman and Fred Olney threshing at Moorhen Farm, Shillington in February 1977.
(Betty Chambers – Meppershall WI; Susan Olney – Tingrith WI)

School pupils in 1965 at Meppershall VA Lower School. Built in the 1840s when the charity school in the village joined with the National School, it was much extended in the 1870s when education became compulsory and again in the 1960s and 1995. A small swimming pool was installed three years after this photo was taken.
(Betty Chambers – Meppershall WI)

Pupils outside Steppingley school, March 1976. The school was built by the Duke of Bedford in 1877, then latterly leased to the County Council. It closed in 1983 and has now been made into a private house.
(Susan Olney – Tingrith WI)

Dinner ladies at Riseley Lower School 1971. The School Dinner Service began in Bedfordshire during the Second World War and was run entirely by the County Council until the mid 1980s when it was contracted out. In this picture Sheila Pope is Cook Supervisor, with Nell DiFolco, Mary Hancock and Mary Roberts as kitchen assistants. They fed 160 children every day – there were no freezers available then and all vegetables were freshly prepared. (Sheila Pope – Keysoe WI)

The Queen visited Bedford in May 1976 for the official opening of the Bedford Modern School. Her programme also included visits to the John Bunyan School and Sports Centre, Puttenhoe Old People's Home, and County Hall. She is pictured meeting residents of Harpur Trust Almshouses. (Sue Howe – Bedford WI)

83

MODERN TIMES

(After 1980)

While out-of-town development has attracted people away from the old town centres and village shops in the last decades of the century, people have become more aware of the need to protect our traditional services and to support those who provide them. The car has changed our way of life beyond recall, but more and more voices are raised against its influence. Like every other county in England, Bedfordshire has suffered from increasing traffic problems, though no sure solutions have yet been found for this blight of modern times. Bypasses have alleviated pressure in some areas, and in the late 1980s the Luton-Dunstable Relief Road was built in an attempt to ease travel in this most congested corner of the county.

Luton Airport has expanded into London's Third International Airport, and into an employer second only to Vauxhall Motors in the county. The opening of the M25/M1 intersection in 1986 made the airport more accessible still. The good effects this has had for local employment have to be weighed against the noise and pollution suffered by residents, but the airport has a proud place in Bedfordshire's history this century.

Bedfordshire is today very much a part of the commuter belt around London, its fast connections by rail on what used to be known as the 'Bedpan Line' when it ran from Bedford to St Pancras station, attracting many city workers. Immigration has created mixed communities in Bedford and Luton, which have experienced their problems, but there are many individuals keen to work towards a true feeling of community in these areas.

Mobile telephones, computers, CD players and videos have come into our lives and revolutionised them in a very short period. Children learn about a world made smaller by new technology, and master skills which daunt their parents. Yet there is a growing desire to hold on to the best of the past – as BT found out when it began removing the much loved red telephone boxes from our streets.

Farming has experienced a decline and more land is being put towards recreational use, such as golf courses. Popular leisure activities include gliding and hang gliding on Dunstable Downs (and more recently, synchronised kite flying!), and water sports on the reservoir at Graffham Water. Bedford Regatta is still held on the river Ouse, as it was at the start of the century. Luton Hoo and Woburn Abbey attract many visitors, and Whipsnade Zoo has developed into a major zoo in its own right. 'Leisure' has itself become an industry.

The Royal Society for the Protection of Birds has its headquarters at Sandy. More attention is being paid to all aspects of the environment and there is a greater awareness of the need to protect and conserve what we have. Local companies have been encouraged to do their bit towards this, especially in the areas of Bedfordshire where sand or chalk extraction could have drastic effects on the environment. Blue Circle Cement have now gone from their works at Houghton Regis, and their old

After 1980

quarry is today a nature reserve.

In the late 1980s storms and hurricane-strength winds that swept across southern England brought a massive loss of trees in the county and widespread damage to property. For a time in some areas the old wartime spirit was evident as people rallied round to help until the over-stretched emergency services could get through.

The 50th anniversary of the ending of the Second World War was widely commemorated in the county in 1995. Street parties recreated the celebrations of VE Day, and many children were bemused by the appearance of long forgotten delicacies such as spam fritters and banana-flavoured parsnip sandwiches!

In 1994 Bedfordshire Federation of Women's Institutes celebrated its 75th anniversary. Amongst a programme of special events, the highlight was perhaps a concert given by the world famous Vienna Boys Choir.

Anne Salmon, WI County Chairman 1992–6, Jennifer Montague and Eileen Parker at Luton Hoo's 'Celebration of Flowers', part of the Federation's 75th anniversary programme. (Photo, courtesy of J. Wood, Herald & Post)

THEN & NOW. The Promenade along the river at Bedford in the 1920s, and today. Though this boatman has gone, the use of the Embankment today is much the same as shown in the earlier photograph. The river still provides boating facilities and residents and visitors alike stroll by the river and enjoy the gardens and the water. There are many lovely trees which have obviously matured since the 1920s.
(Nora Freeman – Ravensden WI)

THEN & NOW. When the river Great Ouse floods between the villages of Carlton and Harrold the roadway, on the Carlton side of the bridge, can be up to two feet under water. At the beginning of the century this traveller (opposite) managed to cross safely in his horse-drawn vehicle. Today local residents watch horseless carriages attempt to do the same, often, much to their enjoyment, failing in the task. The bicycle is one form of transport that can get its rider through the flood – albeit with wet feet! (Mrs E. Lillford & Carole Ryan – Carlton & Chellington WI)

Wrestlingworth Crossroads (known to locals as The Turnpike) disappeared under the snow after a blizzard cut the village off in the 1980s.
(Carolyn Driver – Wrestlingworth WI)

The hurricane that swept over southern England in October 1989 resulted in a massive loss of trees across the county – at Chiltern Lodge in Studham a further storm in February 1990 proved too much for one huge old beech tree. A total of 16 trees were lost in this one garden. Electricity cables were brought down and power was off for 36 hours.
(Anne Salmon – Studham WI)

New roads have often meant the loss of countryside. Here work was in progress on the Shefford by-pass in June 1989, taken from the site of the present roundabout and petrol station. Houses now occupy the field on the right.
(Betty Chambers – Meppershall WI)

THEN & NOW. The Luton-Dunstable Relief Road under construction in 1988, showing the bridge over the M1 being built, and the road as it is today. The row of white houses (centre left) in Bradley Road link the two pictures.
(Angela Brown – Flitton & Greenfield WI)

The demolition of Wootton school in autumn 1996, showing inside the main classroom. The school house is to the right. The school was built in 1877 and last used as a school in 1975 – it had stood empty and unused for 21 years.
(Mrs G. Head – Wootton WI)

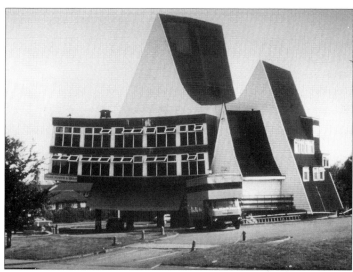

The Windsock public house at Dunstable before it was demolished in the late 1980s. There are now houses and flats on the site, in front of Dunstable Downs and near the Gliding Club.
(Mrs V. Squires – Totternhoe WI)

THEN & NOW. Landmarks disappearing – London Brick Company chimneys at Stewartby Works (opposite) were demolished in the 1980s.
(Mrs G. Head – Wootton WI)

91

Changing awareness of the threats to wildlife have led to changes in our zoos. This was the Dolphinarium at Whipsnade Park in the early 1980s – the dolphins have now been replaced by sealions.
(Angela Brown – Flitton & Greenfield WI)

Some new 'traditions' have taken hold. Every year on Easter Monday the Round Table charity pram race is run by teams of two people from the Commander in Chief pub in Clophill to the Rugby Club in Ampthill – this was in 1981.
(Susan Olney – Tingrith WI)

Above Since the mid 1980s there has been an annual air show at Cranfield. The Red Arrows were photographed in 1994 on the runway before they left to display elsewhere, returning to Cranfield for the finale of a show that lasted nearly six hours and included a 60 minute display by helicopters and an acrobatic display by a glider. The Red Arrows have proved time and again that for precision high-speed flying, they are second to none.
(Angela Brown – Flitton & Greenfield WI)

Old crafts are still in demand. In February 1991 David Kitchener came to layer the hedge around a grass field in which horses and chickens roamed at Park Farm, Steppingley. The farm, formerly owned by the Duke of Bedford, is now run by John Olney as a Bedfordshire County Council tenant farmer. (Susan Olney – Tingrith WI)

Links with farming and the countryside are still important lessons to be learned by the county's children. Wrestlingworth Playgroup visited the cows at Shuttleworth College Farm in 1980.
(Carolyn Driver – Wrestlingworth WI)

George and Bernard Moss, Head Keepers for Mr Charles Williams, Berryshead, with their beaters at Bury End, Eversholt in January 1981. Mr Williams was one of a company who formed Bedford Settlers Estate when the Duke of Bedford had to sell outlying farms to pay death duties in the 1950s. He ran shoots for guests, including Prince Charles and Earl Mountbatten.
(Susan Olney – Tingrith WI)

John Heywood of Wood Farm, Flitwick, with two of his Galway cattle at the South Bedfordshire Show in July 1984. County shows attract people as spectators from all walks of life. The Show has been held at Toddington Manor since 1996 by kind permission of Mr Neville Bowman-Shaw.
(Susan Olney – Tingrith WI)

Below *Still in good working order, Michael Watts' 95 year old steam engine powered the harvesting at Pedley Lane Farm, Clifton in August 1996. It is usually seen now only at steam rallies but proved that it was still capable of taking over from the combine.*
(Photo courtesy of Bedfordshire Newspapers, via Katherine Edwards – Clifton WI)